ROWAN
TREE OF PROTECTION

~

CHRIS HOWKINS

PUBLISHED BY
CHRIS HOWKINS

PUBLISHER
Chris Howkins, 70 Grange Road,
New Haw, ADDLESTONE, Surrey.
KT15 3RH

PRINTED
Unwin Brothers Ltd., The Gresham Press,
Old Woking, Surrey, England.
GU22 9LH

ISBN 1 901087 00 X

CONTENTS

*
***
*

THE ROWAN
THE TREE OF PROTECTION

The two great trees of British folklore that are well known to most people today are the Oak and the Yew but there are two others , far lesser in stature but greater in tradition: the Elder and the Rowan. This little volume brings together those traditions concerning the Rowan which are still remembered today, and to some extent puts them into their historical perspective but this collection is by no means complete and much of the explanations must remain unproven as the story stretches back thousands of years. There is a separate book for the Elder.

The raw material has been collected by the writer from members of audiences when giving talks. therefore it has come mainly from Surrey north east Hampshire, east Berkshire, south west Middlesex (Spelthorne) and south Buckinghamshire but of course the people of those counties have come from far and wide, bringing traditions with them. Certainly much of the Celtic tradition in south east England was supplanted by that of the Saxons, so to extend the content of this volume the reader would do well to hunt in Wales, Scotland and Ireland. It is surprising how much of the Rowan lore is known in the south east and through this we get a glimpse into the past of our ancestors.

First, a botanical note to identify the tree concerned.

WHICH TREE IS THE ROWAN ?

The Rowan tree has also been commonly called the Mountain Ash but this seems to be declining. That, on the whole, is to be applauded as the tree does not belong to the Ash family and therefore the name can cause confusion. The mountain connection is valid in that this tree grows at higher altitudes than other British trees and at the same time keeps a hold on some of the most exposed sites with seemingly little soil, if any.

The Rowan is known by the botanical name *Sorbus aucuparia L.* and it therefore belongs to a very large genus, containing about a hundred different species of deciduous trees and shrubs in the northern temperate countries. The best known species in Britain are the Rowan (*Sorbus aucuparia L.*), the Wild Service Tree (*Sorbus torminalis L.*) and the Whitebeams (*Sorbus aria agg. (L)*) Only the Rowan has pinnate leaves and so has always been distinctive and causes no confusion in its history.

Some species of *Sorbus* hybridize readily and so intermediate forms proliferate. This wealth increases as more different species from around the world are brought into garden and civic use. Natural variation within the species themselves has given rise to a further range of cultivars.

Whitebeam

Wild Service

Nevertheless, the Rowan is a distinctive and popular tree, much used for street planting nowadays as it stays relatively small. It provides amenity value over a long period, from its bright green opening buds through to its flat heads of creamy white blossom. These are followed by bunches of bright orange-red fruits and then reddish foliage in autumn Even the drooping branches of chunky twigs are distinctive against a winter sky.

In old books it will be found under the synonym *Pyrus aucuparia (L.) Ehrh.*

7

The generic
name *Sorbus* comes
from the Latin Sorbum
used by ancient writers like
Pliny and Cato. They used it to
describe the Service Tree but Linnaeus
took it for the name of the whole genus. The
specific name *aucuparia* comes from Continental
languages such as the German but ultimately from the
Latin *avis* for bird and *capere* to catch - because wildfowlers
used the fruits as bait for their nets; thus *auceps* came to mean a
fowler in Latin. The bait was said to work by intoxication,hence
one of its English names is *Cock-drunks*.

IN THE BEGINNING

The story of the Rowan tree, from what we know today, begins in Celtic times, in Ireland. The first people of the Emerald Isle were tribes that invaded from across the seas. One of the conquered groups stayed on as spirit beings. These were the Tuatha Dé Dannan, (pronounced Tootha day danan), meaning the peoples of the goddess Danu. It is these people who dropped one of the sacred red berries from which grew the first Rowan tree in Ireland.

So says Irish tradition as preserved in its literature. That in itself is a wonderful body of work for not only is Celtic literature the oldest in Europe, north of the Alps, but some of its material is so old that it is the only one that gives a glimpse into the Iron Age. It was not written down at the time of course (the oldest document has been dated to the 6th century AD) but its manner of oral transmission from one generation to the next was strict enough for some of the historical narratives to have preserved material which the archaeologists have been able to match with their own findings. The peoples known now as the Belgae, the Gauls and the Damnoni or Dumnonii live on in these tales of old.

These
early people,
the Tuatha Dé
Dannan, became
the gods and goddesses
of the Celts. The transition
from human being to spirit being
while still inhabiting the same world
is something modern readers may
find difficult to grasp. At the end of
life we prefer to think of the human spirit
or soul passing on to another world, whether
it is called heaven, or hell, or purgatory, or what
you will.

The important thing is that the spirits should have a place of their own, separate from ours, and should leave us alone. It is thus a matter of some debate and discomfort that perhaps some spirits linger as 'ghosts'. The Celts had no such problems. As far as we can tell they appear to have viewed life much more as a continuum and therefore both the literature and the archaeological record have failed to yield any evidence for a fear of death. On the other hand there is massive evidence for a belief in another life to come - not so much an *after* life but the *next* life. Therefore the spirit beings are there to observe, to help, and to interfere, in the everyday lives of the Celtic people.

From their literature we know that the Rowan was sacred from the start but we know little else - certainly not the role it may have played in the rituals of these peoples. That is because such information was guarded closely by the Druids who were the custodians of Celtic law and knowledge, and secondly, because all references to worship and sacrifice have been erased from the literature in later times by the Christians. They condensed all the ancestor worship into the adoration of just one man who was transfigured into a spiritual being, Jesus Christ, and focused all the associated tree worship into the veneration of the Cross. Thus from pre-Christian times we are left with supernatural beings with magical powers. Indeed the Celtic name for the Rowan is *fid na ndruad* which means the tree of the wizard.

Thus the early settlers of Ireland were not only defeated by the Goedil or Gaels, to become the supernatural Tuatha Dé Dannan but were stripped of power and purpose by the Christians. They became known as the *aes side* (sing. *sid*). Their home base was believed to be in the prehistoric burial mounds or *sidh* from which comes so much of the folklore of fairy mounds, fairy hills, fairy rings etc.

CHANGE
OF FAITH

So thoroughly did the Christians suppress the sacred Rowan that almost nothing is known about its veneration in pre-Christian times. That thoroughness in itself suggests that the tree was indeed of great importance. Nevertheless, such was the depth of feeling towards the Rowan that it had to be accommodated into the new faith and given a role, although the precise nature of that too has now been lost.

Surely only occasions of deep emotion could have kept alive the lore of the Rowan, such as those occasioned by death. Even if the Celtic people had no fear of death the passing from a mortal life to a spiritual one must have been of supreme importance and indeed the Celtic funerary architecture remains an outstanding testament to that, especially in Ireland.

It may be significant then, that much of the surviving evidence and folklore relates to just that time. Why else is the tree so widely accepted and perpetuated in Christian churchyards from Ireland and Wales to Scotland and Yorkshire? The belief that has devolved to us today is that the Rowans are there to stop the dead from walking. Thus they are not just planted around the churchyard perimeter but can be found on the graves themselves. This, it is still believed, is to stop the spirit of the deceased from haunting it. Rowan twigs were put into coffins or pieces of the wood were built into them, just as they were into the bier for bearing the coffin to the graveside. That is not such an alien idea when after funerals today people can still be heard saying that the deceased "had a good send-off."

If this possibilty that the Rowan was important in the transition from mortal being into spirit being, then its adoption into Chritianity would be most likely (but not undoubtedly) at Easter when Christians celebrate the Resurrection of Christ. Indeed there was an old Christian practice, in Wales, that people marked the Resurrection by wearing crosses of Rowan. This use of the tree and its wood was noted by John Evelyn back in 1644,

"...there is not a Church-yard without one of them planted in them (as among us the Yew) so on a certain Day in the Year, every Body religiously wears a Cross made of the wood."

THE QUICK AND THE DEAD

The possibility that the Rowan was significant for life or the next life is implied by those English names for the tree, which have *quick* in them. This meant *alive;* hence expressions like *the quick and the dead.* Among these names are Quickerberry, Quickbeam or Quickbeam Tree, Quicken, Quicken Tree or Quicken Wood,. Turner's *Herbal* of 1568 refers to,

> "The tree which we call in the North Countrie quicken tre or
> a rown tre, and in the South countrie a quickbeme."

This form was in use by the late Middle Ages but was not new, having evolved out of the Saxon *cwicbeam.* Variants of this can be found in the other languages of North West Europe at that time, indicating a very widespread acceptance of this notion, which presumably dates from the Celtic culture through Europe.

Of course the Celts might not have been the first people to have this idea; they happen to be the first we know about. It should be noted that the Rowan was not the only tree to be so called. Two others were the Aspen and the Hawthorn. The latter is still called the *Quickthorn* by some people and saplings for hedging can still be bought as *quicksets.* This term can include other trees and shrubs used for hedging and for that matter gave rise to Quick Grass for that very lively garden weed, the Twitch or Couch Grass. All these names have the same derivation.

Hawthorn

15

Aspen

When the 'quick' name occurs in a spiritual context though, it seems to be exclusive to the Rowan. That too seems to have evolved in this same magical context, as some people think rowan connects with the Norse word *runa* for a magic charm. Thus Rowan wood is often cited as the material from which to make magic wands - not the rather whimsical things of fiction but items better thought of as staffs of office in early times, rather like a monarch's sceptre, a bishop's crozier, or Black Rod's rod. The magicians of old were the elders of learning but in the earliest literature, such as that from Ireland, where there is a mixture of mortal and spirit beings then the stories can be very entertaining, as when "Étain sat in the chair in the centre of the house, whereupon Fúamnach struck her with a wand of scarlet rowan and turned her into a pool of water."

(From *The Wooing of Étain*; Early Irish Myths and Sagas, trans. by Jeffrey Gantz; Penguin Classics; p.45.)

It *would* be scarlet as the redness was just as magical - just as some think Rowan comes from rune so others see connections with Swedish *ronn* for red, the colour sacred to the gods:

> Rowan trees and red thread
> Hold all evil in their dread.
> or
> Rowan tree, red thread
> Put the witches to their speed.

Fledgeling Blackbird
in Rowan tree. 1982

Thus no common people ate red foods, such as Rowan berries, because they were considered the preserve of the gods. There is a Norse tradition that red was sacred to the god Thor and with it the belief that it warded off all evil forces. Such associations with red can be traced right across Europe to ancient Greece and some of the early invading tribes of countries like Ireland can likewise be traced back to ancient Greece. In Ireland, red thread was supposedly used to bind the Celtic crosses used at Beltine or Beltane - the pastoral festival celebrated on May 1st, at which time the cattle were driven back to their summer pastures. These ancient ideas have persisted until today in that red is still used as the colour of warning. Within living memory it still had a protective role too, e.g. people recall wearing red flannel to cure or ward off fever.

LIFE ON THE LAND

Crucial to life on the land is knowing exactly which land you can take a living from. In the days before maps and barbed wire to demarcate boundaries reliance was entirely upon memory. To prime its accuracy there evolved the practice of 'beating the bounds' whereby the manorial community perambulated the boundaries once a year. The young boys were taken from boundary marker to boundary marker and there flogged with Birch or Willow to make it a memorable spot. The Christian Church adopted this as a way of learning parish boundaries, performing the ritual usually on Holy Thursday or Ascension Day, but the idea goes back to pagan Celtic times, at least. Then it was part of the Beltane ceremonies on May 1st and the boundaries were marked with sprigs of Rowan. in the belief that the Rowan would ward off evil from entering the lands and affecting the livestock.

The Rowan traditions still known today cover a wide range of animals: cattle, horses, pigs and sheep. Even hunting dogs were said to run faster with Rowan in their collars !

Turning attention to the working of the land, for centuries the standard draught animal was the ox. The horse took hundreds of years to win acceptance and never did succeed completely. Tractors were available before the last oxen finished working the land, in the first few decades of this century.

Rowan wood was fasioned into the pegs or pins that fastened the yokes for the harnessing of the oxen, in the belief it would ward off evil that might slow or weaken the beasts. Thus in his *Natural History of Wiltshire* John Aubrey (1626-1697) remembers that in his boyhood the Herefordshire people used the Rowan, or Whitty-tree as they called it, "to make pinnes for the yoakes of their oxen...believing it had the vertue to preserve them from being forespoken [bewitched]." From a practical viewpoint it was a good choice since the wood has a certain amount of 'give' in it, to take the strain, hence whitty which comes from the Saxon 'wic' or 'wice' meaning pliant, as in Witch Hazel and Wych Elm. For the same reason it was used for the spokes of wheels.

There are a number of other references to Rowan yoke pins from the 17th century so at that time it was probably more than just local practice. Similarly, the pliant suckers were interlaced or plaited between the horns of the oxen. Alternatively, Rowan wood was used for making the plough handles, both to protect the ploughman and to drive evil out of the fields. Indeed, the wood was selected for all manner of tool handles, particularly agricultural tools, right up to last century but it seems to have died out now.

Turning from oxen to dairy cows and it is the stalls that are given protection, by nailing up Rowan branches. This was said to keep the spirits from stealing or 'overlooking' [bewitching] the milk. Other trees are recorded being used for the same purpose, including Hawthorn and Wayfaring Tree and a range of herbaceous plants too, of which the White Bryony was generally held to be the most efficacious.

Similarly, Rowan wood was built into butter churns or else the churn staffs and milk stirrers were made of it. There was also the practice of intertwining a branch into a circlet to drop over the milk churns. Again, Hawthorn was used in the same way. The Rowan would seem to be the Celtic choice and the Hawthorn was the Saxon version. The relationship between Saxons, Hawthorn and dairying was very strong, although the significance has by now been lost. This is also said of France where similar practices were known. The alternative to a circlet was to stand a Rowan staff or pieces of branch inside the churns.

From the Scottish Islands right down to Cornwall these various practices played their part in everyday life. No other plant was held in such high regard for protecting milk, even on the days when it was considered to be under the greatest threat, such as at Midsummer. This became the Christian Feast Day of St. John the Baptist and was still the time of the annual blessing of all dairy cattle and dairying activities. Indeed, on that day Rowan was considered even more powerful than the holy St.John's Wort itself (*Hypericum perforatum*). From Devon comes the reassurance that the very presence of Rowan in the dairy was sufficient to prevent the milk

Churns and Staffs.

20

from curdling - a splendid insight into the way our ancestors would blame the unexplainable upon evil forces, whether brownies, witches, little folk, gremlims, call them what you will. Curdling was one of the signs of the milk having been 'overlooked' or given the 'evil eye', and giving something the evil eye was still bringing court action this century.

Horses attracted similar beliefs. Twigs of the tree were tucked into the bridle, to ward off evil, especially at those times when spirit forces were feared of being especially active - usually Midsummer Eve (23rd June) and All Hallows (31st October). In some places at Hallowe'en the twig was fashioned into a cross and such crosses were carried upon the person as well. A second reason for putting Rowan sprays into the bridle was to control a horse that had unfortunately been betwitched. It was supposed to be very calming of all livestock that were restless after betwitchment.

Sheep seem to have been more difficult to safe-guard in these sorts of ways, not only because of their famous unco-operative nature but also no doubt because of their sheer numbers. There were thousands upon thousands in vast flocks in former times. The scarcity of reports that are specific to sheep suggests that they must have relied upon the general rituals that safeguarded pastures. However, the medieval Cistercian monasteries made Yorkshire into one of the great heartlands of sheep farming and from that region comes a variety of rituals concerning several different plants but including the Rowan. Just as Hazel garlands were put round lambs so too were Rowan ones. From Scotland, Lightfoot in his *Flora Scotica* of 1777 recorded that at Strathspey the farmers drove all their sheep and lambs through hoops of Rowan wood on the morning and again in the evening of May Day and then the farmers themselves stepped through it. The ritual was still being reported until last century.

Pigs can be temperamental at the best of times so it's no surprise that they too were sometimes thought to have been bewitched. The fear was, that they would not fatten. The preventative measure was putting a garland of Rowan stems over their head onto their necks but to really ensure that they fattened well they needed to wear a yoke of Rowan. An illustration

22

showing such a yoke reveals how effective that would be! It's not a matter of witchcraft but exercise. The yoke was a stout but pliant Rowan branch placed over the pig's neck with another thinner one passing under the throat so that the projecting ends could then be bound together. Obviously this yoke projected out the sides, making the pig very wide - too wide in fact to break through any gaps in its enclosure and run off its fat. More importantly, it would stop the dash for freedom between the keeper's legs whenever the sty door was opened - anyone who has kept pigs will know the delight that pigs take in this forceful dash between the legs! There is a lot of truth in the expression that a bow-legged man "couldn't stop a pig in a passage" ! Similarly some readers will remember when, at village fetes, you could buy the chance to go into a pig pen for a set time to catch the pig. If successful, the pig could be kept. No pig changed owners that way; they are just too elusive. Thus any pig on the loose would race with delight up and down the street between the villagers' vain attempts to catch it and thereby run off its fat. Yoking pigs would indeed assist control for a lazy fattening life.

Continuing with the idea of fattening livestock, the Rowan has widespread folklore in connection with the gads or goads that were used as driving sticks by the stockmen. This lore, as recalled today, is full of contraditictions. In general, but more so in the north, such sticks should indeed be cut from the all protective Rowan:

Woe to the lad
Without a Rowan-tree gad.

In the south, however, this was the one wood that should *not* be used. It was said to be unlucky or that it would bring out weals on the animal's body. Maybe, just maybe, this arose as prejudice from the Saxons against the older Celtic beliefs that they met with upon arrival in Britain. It is likely that it is the northern or Celtic lore that should be heeded. After all, the tree was not common in the south in those early times but has spread southwards during the time of recorded history.

Furthermore, that protective lore fits the pattern of other uses mentioned, including its service as walking sticks, for which it was believed to be particularly potent at warding off the dreaded Evil Eye. That was feared to be transmitted by any woman caught staring at fattening stock. This applied even if she were staring admiringly and even if the livestock were her own. Getting caught resulted in women being taken to court and such action is recorded from well into the 20th century, as unbelievable as it may sound now.

Similarly:

> If your whipstock's made of Rowan
> You can ride through any town

since such accessories were considered very calming to the horse as well as safeguarding both horse and rider from nearby evil. There are similar beliefs in this category relating to the Elder tree. Carry a piece of Elder into any strange town and you will not be molested. Apparently you won't get saddle sore either!

Claims that all this lore, being agricultural, indicates that the Rowan represents an agricultural or fertility deity, may be stretching the connections too far. Admittedly the Celts were very proficient pastoralists, but, from what is known now, from the ancient literature and from archaeology, the Celtic deities did not have specific responsibilities. This is a notion made familiar from other cultures. Most Celtic deities appear to have been very local in their area of influence. Towards the end of the period, under Roman influence, carved inscriptions can be found and from these we know by name over four hundred such deities. Very few of these seem to have been known at all widely. This just makes the Rowan all the more fascinating as belief in the power of this tree *does* seem to have been widespread. Also, of course, it was so important that still it lingers today.

HOME PROTECTION

Just as walking sticks made of Rowan were considered to be protective so Rowan rods were to be found about a country cottage for the same reason. In particular, they were fixed into openings to bar against any intrusion by evil spirits. These ranged from ventilation appertures in barns, stables and cattle sheds through to the chimney of the home itself. Up chimneys the rods were braced across the brickwork to make a grid as no evil force was expected to pass through such a thing. In Ireland, at least, the Rowan was also believed to prevent the fire from being bewitched, and some readers will remember the vexation caused by a fire that wouldn't 'catch' in the morning. In parts of Ireland this fire protection was specific to 1st May, May Day, but evidently in Yorkshire it was 2nd May when the house was hung with Rowan.

It was also believed that evil would not pass through a circle and so there are records of Rowan hoops being placed around buildings rather than crosses. These may be pre-Christian but crosses are likely to be a Christian adaptation. Alternatively, sprays were hung up over the hearth or over the door. The latter should not be confused with the pieces of bushes, particularly Holly, that were nailed up over front doors to indicate to passers by that there was home brew available for sale within.

Outside the home Rowans were grown as guardian trees and many remain to this day, even if the occupants are no longer aware of these country beliefs. This was highlighted after the Great Storm swept across southern England in 1987 bringing so many trees down. Then householders wondered why the neighbours were so horrified by their fallen Rowan when it wasn't even their's! Many letters and phone calls were received by the writer on this topic. From Holyport in Berkshire came the belief that losing one in a storm was a particularly bad omen. The protection afforded seems to be towards the living occupants rather than the structure or contents. Thus in the south west it is known as 'Care' or 'Care Tree' which is old enough to be traced back to *kerdhyn* in the ancient Cornish language, just as it is *caorthann* in Irish and *Cayer* in West Wales. This protective belief is often linked with the preventing of haunting by the spirits of the dead. Anyone now wanting a Rowan in the garden should be aware that to transplant one is believed to be unlucky! Plant a berry instead; the sapling grows fast. When it's grown big, resist cutting it; for that's unlucky too and so is burning it!

Not only was the tree believed to deter the entry of evil forces but also to appease any upset household spirit or 'brownie' living within, which might otherwise turn into a nasty 'boggart' with which no one would wish to share a home. A contented brownie would (will?) labour all night, free of charge and without complaint. If your household is blessed with such a being, remember that to offer payment even in gratitude, will give rise to major offence and retribution. As a gesture of your appreciation it is advised to put down a saucer of milk before going to bed. The brownies will not touch it but will note your gesture with pleasure. This was still being done in Sussex in 1964, Berkshire in the 1970s and Surrey in 1989. There are even later dates for other safeguarding rituals concerning the Little Folk.

CHILDHOOD

Rowan was also used to protect a mortal's spirit from an untimely 'passing over' to the other side. Obviously this applied particularly to young children, bearing in mind the high rate of infant mortality. Thus babyhood was a time of great concern, with Rowan having a number of associations with cradles. A Rowan twig under the bottom blanket in the cradle will deter the Devil from sleeping on the baby's face and suffocating it. Another version collected recently has such a twig deterring the Devil from pinching the baby black and blue all over until it dies. These sound like explanations for what we would now call 'cot deaths'.

Once rockers had been invented for the cradle (in later Middle Ages) it was said that to make them out of Rowan wood was just the thing to keep the baby safe - the Devil would never stand on such wood in order to climb in. Cradles made of wood, as opposed to woven wickerwork, were to have pieces of Rowan incorporated so as to protect the baby from all harm - a notion known in America too. Hanging a sprig over the top of the cradle or hanging it on the end is also claimed to be efficatious. These practices must have evolved in post-Celtic times as they imply a fear of death. Certainly the personifying of evil forces as 'The Devil' must be from later Christian times.

BEWARE OF MIDSUMMER

Continuing with the Little Folk, evil forces, faeries, witches, or whatever, then it was Midsummer (24th June) when these were considered to be especially active. This was so even after the suppressing work of the Christian Church, which had to sanctify the day as the Feast of St. John the Baptist. Similarly, one of the most powerful of the pagan plants had to be Christianised as St.John's Wort (*Hypericum perforatum*) Even more powerful was the Rowan and came to be used to ward off evil influences at this time.

It was believed that these spirit beings lived in the ancient burial mounds (barrows etc.) which in Ireland are the 'sidhe' (or 'sidh', pronounced 'she') while in Scotland they were called 'shian' From all over the British Isles , however, there are associations between faeries and what are now called archaeological monuments, such as barrows, standing stones, stone circles etc. Where there were no such focal points then hilltops were viewed thus instead. These places, we are warned, must be avoided and no more so than at Midsummer. There are countless tales of people being whipped away for a night of music and dancing and merrymaking, ending the next morning with a cold dew-sodden confused wakefulness, often breathless from dancing and excited by half remembered wonders. Writers have certainly enjoyed all this when they trivialised the faeries into fairies , put wings on them and crushed their reality between the pages of children's fairy tale books.
This is not the place to discuss this further but to say that anyone trapped in a fairy ring could be pulled free by mortals on the outside holding a Rowan branch across the ring for the captive to grab and be hauled out. Wearing a Rowan cross safeguarded the rescuers.

MAY EVE AND MAY DAY

Again it is the Celtic regions that appear to have made greatest use of the Rowan at this time. The Germanic peoples (Saxons etc.) used Hawthorn. In the Celtic calendar this festival was Beltane and was important because they were (in Ireland at least) a pastoral society based upon cattle rather than an agrarian one with crops. Indeed the wet climate of Ireland is not ideally suited to cereals but encourages pastures and it was to these that the cattle were moved from their winter quarters at Beltane. Thus a lot of the folklore relates to cattle and was presented above.

As far as crops are concerned, Rowan branches were put among them to ensure a good harvest. This is noticeably Celtic for the Celts believed that if they practised the correct rituals ahead of maturation then all would be well. Consequently they had no 'harvest festival' in the sense of giving thanks for a harvest. A good harvest was only to be expected after the rituals.

In Christian times when May Day celebrations were still held the Rowan was just one of dozens of plants employed, indoors and out. Tying with red thread perpetuated the sacredness of red though the connection seems to have been largely forgotten.

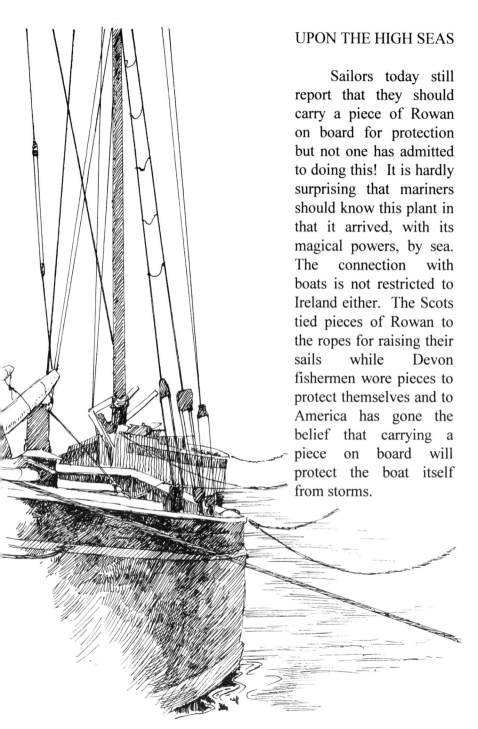

UPON THE HIGH SEAS

Sailors today still report that they should carry a piece of Rowan on board for protection but not one has admitted to doing this! It is hardly surprising that mariners should know this plant in that it arrived, with its magical powers, by sea. The connection with boats is not restricted to Ireland either. The Scots tied pieces of Rowan to the ropes for raising their sails while Devon fishermen wore pieces to protect themselves and to America has gone the belief that carrying a piece on board will protect the boat itself from storms.

INDEX OF OTHER PLANTS

INDEX OF MAIN THEMES

****

FOR A LIST OF OTHER PUBLICATIONS OR A LIST OF TALKS GIVEN
TO GROUPS, WRITE TO: Chris Howkins (Publications), 70 Grange Road,
New Haw, Addlestone, Surrey. KT15 3RH
****